Book of Mother

By the same author

Book of Mother

Christopher (Kit) Kelen

PUNCHER & WATTMANN

First published in 2021
Published by Puncher and Wattmann
PO Box 279
Waratah NSW 2298

http://www.puncherandwattmann.com
puncherandwattmann@bigpond.com

ISBN   9781922571274

Cover design by Miranda Douglas
Typesetting by Morgan Arnett
Printed by Lightning Source International

A catalogue record for this book is available from the National Library of Australia

Australian Government

Australia Council for the Arts

This project has been assisted by the Australian Government through the Australia Council, its arts funding and advisory body.

for my brother, just the one

I wonder what was the place where I was last night.
                                                     — Amir Khushro

Come build in the empty house of the stare.
                                                     — Yeats

Dementia is living the dream.

one more wonder

all the birds have flown
into the tree

are a knot
then let

it's grey for drab
not seen before

won't it be rain
for telling the roof?

that one's soft
but this is softest
one's beautiful

her, not her
and if not, who?
whom?

things are
on the blink
in my mother's garden

these were the first eyes

this was my breath before
and skin from

I too wrinkle up with

remembering before one's time

comes at the end of years

I couldn't sit

the milk is off
no nose for

woke from this
but hadn't slept

I don't recall
what I dreamt

I hadn't slept
at all

stage four border five

it's the words under the words

it's not what anybody meant

    the twenty nine schoolgirls spent the night in the house
    they were invited
    no harm done

    where did they stay? I'm not asking

    there's an unravelling
    the light shines through

    too late when you think of the thing

    you can't ask anyone else to do it
    have to take yourself out
    do it while you can

here in a death of years

a midden
good honest
podiatry
the special socks
(as advised)

things hidden
and things hide themselves

the paper comes
and can unwrap
the headlines
now beyond
no longer read

first asleep and fast
it's like the sky's in things

ave!

hail full of grace
one flown

forget the words
I am not here

it's not with words
to know

it was a church
hail mother was

choir fire
so sings to me

the brightest paint is sunshine
the bluest sky clear air

time runs out
drips from

best slept

tin skin
up flimsy
sings

hail for history
one gone
the shell beyond
shows egg

forget the words
all best unsaid

it's what you taught me
with your eyes
when once I came
to world

Peter Rabbit

on Military Road, the library

there is a first light
not twice the same
goes with us unsaid

mine retains
each step upsy daisy
rabbits bounce

read to me
I lack the letters make the words
point to tell now

street and car, splinter
coming up
the white paint stairs

hand held to voice
where wonder, remember
long before the map

and still looking
I can't find the book
that we're in

I've never seen one of them before

a little weather in the viciously rain
and stays where it's supposed to be
not pouring in
what's thing over the top
let out the smoke?
big saucepan under that to catch
under the drop pot thing
I've always been home when the big storms come
all halfway ready to go shopping
I'm almost dressed right now

obey a pain

then cloud upon cloud
mist bitten
made ghost

winter comes into these bones

music comes to me
and all afloat

not so far down we're stone

you know the trees
are reach touch
and all take time

you were in the other
when this one was waking

what are the odds of us then
...are the chances we are?

first thing up rotate a sphere
it's date line and equator

the everywhere ache
is winter got in

take the pill
and swallow
it down

to sneeze at

to get her to the doctor's

because we, every one of us, must go
we are fit as a fiddle too
and where is that bruise from?
the itch
because there might be a reason
exactly! *because* you can't remember
we have to check to see
because the doctor will know
you don't want to get the flu
the doctor called and asked
because there is an appointment now
these things have to be tested
it's not very far and we're taking you
you don't want to disappoint people
because it is a fact of life
and at your age
yes that's it
and no, you really are
we don't know either
it's been a long time since you went
it's just a necessary thing
the others do
we all must
going now
you're coming too

because we love you, mum

some things long since known

the ones on the lawn
tree of its birds

and I was born here
in the cellar

grandfather gave me this place

truth's the new thing every day
else why the paper landed?

I make a blank face
then nobody knows what I want (when, why)

let me write it then we'll always know
someone must have thought that
otherwise how
all wrapped in plastic

what day?
what time?

weird, like a holiday, since

is the plumbing in the tree?

how did it get there?

the past like a puppy
and we're the stick fetched

calendar winks
over at

music listening for us
someone sings
radio gives voice
weather for instance just

a clock is always there again
and never was before

the plumbing's in the tree, mum
because I put it there

I didn't really get to meet those people

housekeepers had cleaned it up
beds were made neatly

don't know who chose them as the chosen people
to sleep in that room
I've been back for a week
don't know whose those kids were

the cleaners
they call it mum's secret formula
I'll tell you
tell everyone and anyone
one cap of the bottle
furniture oil
and the same amount of what's it called (?)
eucalyptus
I don't know who told me about the secret formula
years ago
I don't think the mail's come yet today
who is it out there now?

thieves have broken in

and they have left a language
mustn't go past my letterbox
mustn't onto the street
without somebody looking after me

they think I'm going to fall over in the mud
it doesn't worry me
I like to go out with someone

I can't see the (street) sign from there

says
come along with me a little further
I can't remember here

cicadaly loud

an age of falling
jacaranda strew
like the country between ears
day spilt

guesses
and tricks of the way
less more
seasons of vanish
cicadaly

wrung from the heat?
don't they tell out breezes?
rhythm though singing

no, otherworldly

imagine a silence in the after storm
webs swept

I know they are building
their civilization on ours
on top
it's tilted
they shell out for this

veined wings
proud squat
so soaring
sit and spit

heard
but what you see is an absence

they come with a simple message
    to deafen
oh when will we understand?

look back far enough
17 Avenue Road

almost to before I was
and a kind of Christmas to come
...who knows?

elevated view from the backyard
step round the fence side
goanna tail gone, was it?
under the house
lived where the mildew was
uniform exhumed
so to commit
forget the war

then other side, legend of the rooster
died of old age because nobody could...

and centre of the backyard
next to that 44 gallon fire
under mulberry

there was time before we were digging to China
top of a bank
and behind that, what?
Percy, I believe
blue over
harbour summer stillness out

look far enough into yourself, who else?
back there are things you can almost see
wild wind-up toy
so much of the action lino-level

laundry where the mulberry wine blew
ceiling as purple as dad's office shirts
line under the silk worm farm –
was it a Hill's Hoist?

came round
bob a job
and letterbox bungers
some lost their eyes back in the day

no one said that then
but you could see it coming
all this legend
the shears go click
then decimal – hope dashed
in the possum shine of a cent
so tiny and run up a tree

Uncle John took his brows off in the war
making a bomb in the laundry
bushy ever since his little war effort
…boys will be
(lung cancer much later
and named a guitar after him
… he taught us flok
when flash flood filled
the pool with mud)
…

where was I then?
round round
tickle you under

eyes at their clearest
in through to the kitchen
where my brother did the harbour on cupboards
remember a simmer
and out of doors
down by where the tram lately

bottletops, splintery rails
grimey bob and diesel choof
no one would swim in that harbour now

and later, cot at Mrs Monaghan's
was forty winks
...ran away from once
right past there to Calypso St

buried the lettuce sandwiches
in the sand at Auntie Basie's
that was the hysterectomy time
or so I later learned
no one would ever do lettuce to me
(father would defend, mum said)

through palings to the next door kids
can't think of a name who they were

Uncle George had those beetle crates for cubbies
splintery as well but did
and he had me up shoulder high
once on that scary bridge was enough
have I recovered?
you ask yourself
nor praise nor blame

that was all elsewhere
let's have the backyard back
slope with pink bubbles, a vine
and the garden furniture I still see
we took it with us, painted it later
was it bright yellow before?

these are things the sunshine did

but round a sort of corner, I believe
and must have been a pantry
big cupboard, was it, at the back?

telephone there somewhere
black, letters and numbers
I was ringing information – find out stuff
…height of a mountain
I was ringing the Patent Office
with regard to the pom-pom mobile

must have been a room off to the side there

what good humour everyone had
so many steps to the letterbox
rough stumbling too
and underfoot consider then

Charming was taken by cocker spaniel thieves
or might have been King Charles

later Cappy who would irrigate dad's trousers
home from the office
so happy to see him

have I mentioned Mr Murphy?
mongrel stayer (or I will)
who caught the ferry
one day sadly...

up the back was, you remember
codger botherer turned off the water
to us just because he could
or else it was a grudge to tell
some thing beyond my years

I remember writing out the letters
from the newspaper
on the side of the newspaper
that was on the floor
in front of the telly
on which JFK was shot

or there was the plumber coming in
when I was on the throne
(invention of mortification)

was that Memory #1
or just what I was told?
(the way a pet's attributed thoughts, opinions
... that's how it begins)

gunbarrel hall
and dad with the samurai sword defending
it's all in *The Man from Overdraft*

burnt my bum on that stove

planets all mote-afloat in a beam
still in bed
till pancake

looking back, hard squint
it's not as if you come to a wall
not life to flash before
this is out of endless time...
the years until dinner

you'd think you could see further in
but days were seasons then
weather supernatural

all bets set my head on a certain track
a thread and carried it
round with me

the typewriter of legend
high on a desk in the growing out view
on which I am said to have played

what a distraction I was am and will be
not least to myself these days

usually someone knocks on the doorbell

and a hand comes in and takes me
with what I've got
a knock on the Monday morning

coming!

down the stairs
no nightie and slippers

dad at the end

someone told me a terrible thing –
that he was gone
my husband

it's just a theory, you know

it's by stages
as if you were emptying out of a cup
and someone asked
'how much left today?'

rabbits on the lawn at St Ives

mother wants to stay in the house
she believes that there are many
that this is to trick her

which one is mine?
where did I stay last night?

I'm right down at the bottom
right down

you're in Sydney

oh I'm beyond Sydney

past that

where?

hang on and I'll look out the front and tell you what the street is…

*

two brown rabbits on the lawn

from a distance
they are some kind of test

they are a message

in which dimension are they?
do I believe?
and what do they teach us here?

the Woolstore Australian Made All Schools Botany Book 1966

go back to the crooked line
to the jagged star
map of Christmas

Pitter and Patter were two little raindrops
a plum rolled down the hill

all these states
where did I stop to draw?
and why?
how did a line take off?

so many countries our Commonwealth is
often the spelling is odd
you can't hear

my dictionary began with
A baby
then we went on to Beef
and Beet is a vegetable
Bent is a kind of curve

things that flew

times tables
ten was a synch
        a cinch
        sinch

so many things invented then
not least the Pom-Pom-Mobile
(more later, some before)

a lovely pair of Japanese slippers
I, quite correct in anatomy department

not a thing glum
but where was my best work?

from smoke as ink
we somewhere rise

radio so few jingles
way to school through the unbuilt bush
webs there, watch out too
mean spiders

there had to be a stillness
winter made it far

sat on the heater first to arrive
only the queen could see

I knew the world
a beautiful place
the beautiful place
for me

do I know you?

what are we here for?

what's the program?
what's next?

I know this won't complete
not quite an idea

how did we get?

I do know you,
don't I?

I'm me
you're you

that's straight

reprise
or
last laugh of the living

she was a helper
straight bat
cursive

unlike dad
you could read what she wrote
accounts would keep her up

she was often uncredited editor
payer of bills
nurse to the man laid up with
shrapnel
malaria
organs to go

she was a brush and oil

bounce in the cot
and beads to part
she was the day got up

no knowing where we would go next

can't have always been lost in the bellow
in the moo
ran around after us once

the keys are gone again

anyone forgets that kind of thing

it's not what you see
it's what you know

they went
like nobody's business

where will we find them now?

in dreams they are not gone

where we have been before
sometimes hang on a question

everyone's to visit
it's always neither day nor sleep

but called to conversation
and wander on alone

we're naturals
none tell a lie

still shallow
won't see wings

in dreams they are not gone
take testament

as if you painted with a garden
live out beyond ourselves

there are no numbered years
free, true

you'd never know
you'd never know we were there

tectonic forces

still birth
might have been a fantasy
hard to tell

a grand beginning
by palanquin
as concubine
that's mind's eye
or
she has a palace
in her
the harem in the girl

and hummed a tune
danced to here

there isn't a church to have hung around
there's no one
there's nothing
nowhere to confess

common sense takes hold
we'll have none of that now

her not her

a ghost got in
I repeat myself

monster
won't stop

everything echoes
long way down

here's her stick for pointing
watch out!

falling all ask

who built the cliff?
who wove the net?
who took the push to shove?

so blame?

a little creature says
no one's listening now

it's not her

in the eye
and under speech
never a wink
but

nothing to be done

for what you can't say

starts with walking in

each room tells another time
facts of a matter are close to

we're not the ones who've been here
but you can imagine belonging

all the clocks go
you expect to see dragons
no such thing
in the mirror but
that was the year I was born

have I ever been before?
in one room
how things were left
another still to do

I come out as far
as the day is up

a little bird flew through
to the letterbox

in one room
and you won't tell what door it has!
I think I could know it once

my motherwork

is where I'm from

didn't we read the puddin' together?

and Alice with Auntie Eve

once, unlike Albert, I was on a lead
so never stolen

but somewhere over the rainbow we went
that was proscenium arched – the Orpheum
colour was already known
just like peanuts
sixpence worth
shone silver gone
GI fizz in a bottle

we had a high street
the bus broke down
but anyway we got home

cruel eyes the tiger on the wall
cruel eyes belonging to
all for love

solemnly hilarious
        our agonistics were

and all of it's remembered

stir
it won't ever come to the boil
but cut-and-come again

there's nothing left to do but

I will be sad
I'll cry
when you're gone

for why we can't know
for the one who is with us but

a bending to be told
it was like that

these two
and that's the way they went

what is it from the eyes?

to dark
or light
all one

what if it's me too?

where on earth will we go
if no one remembers here?

in a waiting room

to make you happy
for your own good
because we love you
because I can't explain

won't remember your hand was held

in yellow light
dinosaurs confer
smoke clouds them
or at cards

here elephants trumpet about
giraffe pokes in a head

stood by the fire
too close
to beginning

peg in the board where everyone fits
that was my Day at the Zoo

forget a thing and it's gone

one day I forgot the key
every door was open

forgot aeroplanes
the sky was just blue
wings from before
like insects

forgot my glasses
I could see it all clearly

I knew what had become of me
because I am coming to this

disease makes poetry

let me tell you so that you will forget

that is the beautiful thing
so we can say again, again

it's a fire to sit round
and rotate like planets
seasons for surprise

I have to forget
to be worried with that

only visiting

see in their moment
a long way past

in with the chickens
are they?
strange fluffy

what was there?
you are

might have been yesterday
we were

look up
and gone

we only came to vanish
everyone does that here

inglorious

among the bung ones
all this trinket fiddle
some euphemise for tea

a winter cough would take them off

once in a world change
stride
what bearing!
and bearing into this!

the love of them for us
ours now
spring autumn come around

I have seen them
myself feeble with
sad into those eyes
so seeing

we sing a song
for words from you
'aeroplane jelly for me'

they know more than the tree does
less than the possum to climb

there isn't an end to wish for here

are they alive?
they are

like looking for a mad woman's washing

there are copies
everywhere
as in, for instance, thing in the mirror
or me

as if we had been
brought to life

every animal is
down we wind
to market
and all the way home

count them

potion come to
the toy

as a god revered
once forgot

imitations of something dashed off

we let light in
we let it out

there is some kind of tail in the creature

clothes maketh the man

a lucid interval

while I was looking for a word
I think the page must have turned

when I was in Paris...
when I was in Rome...
when I was in San Francisco...

for all of my persuasions

the weak
the vulnerable
are dedicated in a work
they won't get the voice
you'd be a fool not to see yourself so

you're not the one you think you are

there will be after us all

how many wills did I make?

no one knows

it will be known

just having a bit of fun

the first cup of coffee four times now

but this house has no cellar, mum
I remember the day we moved in

dad – he worked hard
he was your husband

and you too
it was how we could be here
        it was 1966

your grandfather died before this house was built

I haven't had one yet today

        and a new coffee too, that's sly
        we have to get some decaf in

        the book is like time is all over the place
        you will have noticed by now

determining competence

she reached out

it was a real gold coin –
St George and the dragon

it was shining
she reached out

before that is all that
grandfather was
and I can remember his name

but if you keep eating there's nothing

what do you call these things?
oranges, I suppose

this is an old fashioned
of soap

*

so many houses the same they must have built
and why? what good could it do?

questions need to be asked
and asked until answered

the world's no longer sensible
this kitchen I'm in now is identical

and that is just for instance

feet up over the garden
by way of veranda
with what we know

what we can work out

always one more wonder

Bobok

here are the dead
they have a home

screen larger than life
a planet rolled on

some are loud
and some are wild

some deep in

grave to grave
they go

little beans —
that's how they mean

a word
in confidence
with you

this is as far as stretch

the little ones come to join us

happy birthday

bitter in the salad here

takes teeth to catch the mush

no one else has put them anywhere mum

you're the one who doesn't know where they are

everyone else doesn't know where they are
because you don't know

I don't know where they are mum

they must be where you put them

in the madhouse

here's shit woman
always offering

go out on something soft you won't feel
into a box in the ground

here's the screamer
and the one who scolds
the one who'll take your food

we can be smoke too

sullen nurses are all come from wherever
because we placed a dollar lovely
in this trap

wars are to flee, you know

you have to have wished a way here

we are only along for the ride
we're a silence

no one will remember my cruel remarks

the test is the code
or other way

we're visiting

like truth to its acre
far far off
the better things we do

you asked

she is gone
she is still with us

if I ever go gaga
she said

brother!

I want to ask again about when you met dad

why did I never meet my grandfather?

there's no one telling

brother!
all these questions

it was too late when I started

no one to ask this now

she is still with us
she is gone

good for a woman of my years

that's what the doctor has always said
and said for years

as good as can be expected
that's what the doctor still says

when once princess young

and little sistered
as if to coronation, on the way
borne bridal, black and white
(de Groot carved aunty's table legs)
fresh as the diesel whiff harbour
and over a ferry goes

Mr Murphy – the dog – commuted
less fatefully, till he didn't come back
the city was all characters
and mum could water-colourize
or even canvas oil

after the genderless eyes
and goo-goo
girl was a doll in her mirror
boy explorer

the green grass was bamboo
and round the drum fire

mulberry our Tyrian purple
for office shirts

patrician place
because lizard alongside

and Percy over the back fence
for spite, just when you wanted a shower
no one will ever know why
…and I suspect he didn't

dad's uniform rotted under the house
later we got the buttons

there was that chook in the back yard no one could kill
and once the idea of a goat

Wince-alot and Bobo and one
with whom the robbers made off

gets like a remembering
all this

march over the hills and far away
(that's with Grainger, another Percy, one of ours)
there was the hole we were digging
to get to the other side of the world

the radio tuned into
every season come

you have hidden them

I don't know why

is what's lost
hidden
?

is hidden
lost
?

why do you repeat what I say?

everything is gone in the mirror

they are where they were left
will we be left?

if I knew where they were, mum
I would tell you

if I knew where you had put them
I would tell you

you are making me repeat myself

it is you
who have hidden things
I still don't know why

but I do know why you don't remember
and I know I must not say

green capstan in the ashtray burns

and dad's amphora
like a little engine
run around the house

I sat up on the typewriter

life best then was processional
or music struck us up

closest they ever came to divorce
was – once before they were married
that was over the lottery they never ever won
and the other time?
was when mum disinfected dad's pipes

we buried Uncle Jack
and ransacked great grandfather's house
retrieved *Arnold's First German Primer*
lots of bible stories
and *Young Australia*

the adoration of the March fly
in an orchard afternoon

a very nice man who did the garden once

but it seems to stay done
it's strange
he just mowed it

went to school with you or the other one
did the whole job and it only had to be done the once
it stayed done
put a good day's work onto it – hard yakka

come to a puzzle
and then you ring
the number's always there

*

there isn't a moment to be in
they paid in shekels in the Bible
that must be a while back now

she is where the days have gone

carmelite

absolute plain

a white handkerchief
and that was all you were allowed to bring
that was something to give
useful
and not 'a vanity'

she didn't have the vow of silence

but you'd turn the thing around
and it's come out at the other end

there wasn't much sound though

you know what you called
I've forgotten it's —
cross my heart and hope to die —

well not if I can help it

and father in a room with silence

that was God's way in

to a universe of so much to adjust
everything talked round
and the kettle too full
and the tea cup
why was it left half?

the light's on there
don't trip in the dark

don't you like your message mixed?

these were the first eyes catching mine
and skin from
this was my breath

lacks patience for a cup of tea

like it was with Uncle John
can't stop
won't stop
the talking is never going to stop

he was a nuclear physicist
Sydney Hospital too
think pig

they want to take it all away
house and money and me
as if this world were ending so fast
and faster still

where other lives get on
everything has to be said

I have a disappearing mother situation

must find her hiding place

in a pocket
we vanish together

none of it means a thing
quite right to be afraid

communion

at community care
they won't have her on the bus anymore

they bring in the schoolkids for mass
this will be the last time

and she faces the priest
for all to see, to hear

it's bullshit
don't believe him
what he's saying is bullshit

mum's my hero now

ghost in the machine

hungry always, can't get warm
air's empty
someone's in the glass

tap at the window again
knowing she must be there

the little winged thing
squeak
who's that?
mater, you in there?

she's back

still dreaming
wraith-in-life
and risen from the bed

no challenge

you don't get out of this chair

same story over and

kicks legs for figure of fun

like an echo
she haunts herself
hams it up as well

we're the unintelligible
near enough or far

she is cashless like the queen
but she remembers the will
she will be gone

she played a game
and we don't know
nobody does now
I can't see how she wins

I'd like a little chime to tell
it's as if sunshine struck
but I wasn't there

there were no events

just when you think the fire's right out
eyes light, no words — but here's a spark

there won't be any running off
for zombie apocalypse mummy

came back
just a glimmer
and gone

forgetting together could be who we are

mother's method of broadcasting
was to throw the seeds about
when weather was on the way

cuttings too
clippings

dad let the block grow from the edges in
when he died mum took it all back

then you could see
the house from the street
street from the house

it was different when dad was alive
when mum was a going concern

we mourn those here not with us today

whom we may say are still
like in Tanah Toraja, where they keep you upright
in the living room with cigarettes and party snacks
till the family can afford to bury

how many places the lost thing is not!
almost everywhere in fact
why not in fiction?

no, we may not say!

we are writing this down before we forget
today is Tuesday
today is the 8th
I'd put down the time but it's gone

everything will be taken from us

the faces, names
secrets and the shapes of days

news, a trot around the block
lean to the fence for chat

roof over head, all the accounts
the trusts, the emergency stash

our health, our hearts
pretending the breath by bone

everything will be taken from us
from me, from you, from all

every last share is salvaged
nothing ever returned

would one be right in the head
not to fear

property, liberty, happiness —
a life is mourning

it will be taken from us
our say, our vote
haircuts and your spectacles
character
(though it's nothing personal)

all things and thoughts to be equally gone

the fourteen billion years since the Big Bang
four billion years of our sun yet
all the scales of time will be taken

someone will tie off your tongue
the itch will be nothing
dinner and dreams
skin that you're in

we will be bung and gone
in that order, or it hardly matters

the hand to hold
the jaws till teeth

taken from us
truth, the little lies
the big ones

all our goodness
all our woe
it will be taken

a desperation for the facts

all the world goes
when we do

all the world gone
when we are

it's too cold, it's too dark, too dangerous

you'll catch your death of
mad to go out on a night like this
to go over there
to drive anywhere

no good setting out in the morning
only a few hours of light

if the weather's not here yet
it's coming
you bet

you won't get far
not with that equipment
it's like when you were very little
still running away from...
why?

guess it's just how you were made

now tail between legs
let's fold you up in the picnic blanket
bundle you into the stove
it's warm there, you'll be cooked in no time
it's only love that says these things

my little cup cake

who put you up to this?

like fun
lost lore note for those to come

meant no, you won't
not putting up with

steer mum away from a pub smelling door
never know what pours out

like nobody's business
is fast

like fun
it was to be with her

when young
and she gave chase

like fun
could simply be a scoff

Job had patience
Moses took tablets
Noah kept his sarcasm
where it wouldn't get wet

too much milk
so a little pump
she expresses herself

and I have her blue eyes

later steer her
away from a bottle

she was a kindness
to children once

you could be skittled
trust no one

this is one
for the dictionary of mum

# of course remember what you should have done

for a while there were two
and one could love

what a word
and we're with it

there was the snarling
same thing again, again, say

sun shines
so the kettle costs nothing

others see the house is burning
what was it I switched on?

once when I was three

someone chucked me into the deep end
all these years later you think revenge
but who is there?

my mother was a good swimmer
and brothers and sisters and cousins and

it was at Drummoyne
pool on the edge of the river the harbour the water I think
I was about three at the time
you can't expect me to remember much
probably I didn't know the words

if someone is hearing this

and
if I have the
what do you say
whatever it needs to get a ticket on this bus
have to know
when it goes where it goes
and if it's a price I can manage

starts just the single pigeon pottering upstairs down

not so strange to have words with yourself
if you live alone mostly

pee-your-bed
that's what the flower was called
that's what we said to stop them picking the flowers

I'm going to the kitchen
make a cup of coffee for me

what's all this water in the thing
did I do that or did you?

let it go
what's all this cold water for?

will I sleep in this house for the rest of my life?

if you don't know, who knows?

who's in charge?

she imagines someone who isn't me

my mother cannot think of me
it's too late for that

I am two different people
one good, the other is plotting
I have two names too

who's sad? who knows?

it's true I am keeping this dossier

as if disappearance were apotheosis
surely that is no less mad than the two of me?

this is my mother here
like the middle bedroom
waiting to be put away
my mother is still at home

imagines herself – it's not her

there's her hero bastard father

this house her grandfather gave her
she was born at the foot of stairs
in the basement

great scholar
gentleman, knew Hebrew, Greek
said if a man wants to marry you
watch how he treats the waitress
…later on that will be you

she is imagining me
I'm there but she imagines
it can't be me she sees
I'm no longer a topic at all

she grabbed at that sovereign
should tell you something
grabbed it and held on

grim

each word each thing forgotten as said

as sung
forgotten as
you're disappearing

the words of every sentence cling, fit
they are the raft

it's like the dream gone into

and things that are true there are so for how long?
    how long in the dream?

    can't see you anymore

    we time the circle closing

    down to much less than a minute now
    this is living the dream

house without mother
in a Sydney mist

is it time foretold?
here and she's not cause
the flies rub greedy hands
meal's spoiled

she wasn't herself
not in a right mind then
aren't all wounds that way?

is anyone surviving
so far down among the echoes?

we haven't yet taken the last clothes to Vinnies
we've only half been through the books
there's to libraries and archives yet
there's so much not knowing what

it is a burden, this house
signs strange again
plumbing's half bung

we swim through the years here
lazy with what has to be done

so much self belief won't vanish
you have to take it away in a truck

his stoicism
her agitation
a little opera on all hours

I was always escaping
at the very least packed to go

she was a record stuck
one waiting
never out of nightwear
Cassandra of the Top of the Stairs
and Hanrahan said all

then ready to go out
always up for a drink
smokes she left overnight

we are all elsewhere ghosts
sat on a step and learned to spell
Aphrodite for instance
you tie your own laces already

mid sixties tiling perfect still
but now no parquetry protector
the horror for estapol gone

see those two boys weeding the lawn
yes, it was that kind of a camp

here's a huff
there goes the creak
of stairs come up

a shuffle
that's how the cards fell out
a slouch where dad would stretch

cocktails up and down
black forest cake, trifle
rice pud with the damned sultanas

have to pay people to get rid of this stuff
you do know that?

dad was here a long time gone
she had us all talked into a corner
won't be coming back
we'll empty this house of us all

she

who had supernatural powers
who knew what Christmas wanted
what naughtiness was and was not

she who said wait till your father gets home
she who was a step before
could spell every word there was
and we could add things up together
she, once bitten, of sharp words
of the gentle harangue
don't drink from a bubbler, cause dogs

once bright of the dance floor spun
of the tune stuck ages before I was
and sung out over the line   make Monday
the mangle, remember? (as neighbour is to fence!)
far and away, yet with us
she who could hear a joint being rolled a suburb away
she of preternatural olfaction
prognosticator of clouds

whose ancestors were a particular greatness
grandfather – founder and benefactor
and Mary, Queen of Scots

churns, bottles, horsedrawn still
and wash your hands from the dunny
who'll cough up this week?
but everyone had nothing then
father was at sea

wild animal of the virgin ages
before the first tree fell

she saw this little bear asleep
bore silly sausage tantrums

she, pictured before all monuments
ad infinitum Europe,
more continents than we knew then
oblivious to heard it
she, keeper of close secrets, how many of them made up?

construer, exegete

hems up
took in, let out
she of the sewing machine on the dining room table

now of the blank empty stare
she who was always ahead of the game
eyes ears

and in the garden
drawn by dog
or round the block

who never swam
not in my life
who loafed around in a stain
and blamed the beach for glare

she of the early hours
and the Sunday sleep in
have we mentioned pancakes?

Mercurochrome she and Savlon
font of remedies

of the great household health crises
Home Doctor consulted, house call presaged
foreteller of blood poisoning (!)
and ptomaine... voices
of a famine once, avatars of a thirst

she of the tribe survived
she, last of siblings, first among them
boss of and scholarship girl

of roses and thornstuck
of the broken glass through thong
in the high grass should have been mown
and in the surgery waiting, with blood

and me there, with the needle, run off
and later, so patient, having been told
no one could see I'd been done

she of wise saws, melodious snatches
and lyrics lost
first among princesses once

pyjama selector – o intimate mine

Depression minded
suspicious milk was watered
snow droppers or anyone
could strip your line

who'd never trust a tradesman
watch where they go
she of the locks changed later
again and again
of the documents re-written
she with the evil solicitor

of the secret womb removal

of mercy mild once
and inwardly Irish
who sent me to the Church of England scripture
so as to avoid persecution

of growing pains detected
of 'you'll grow out of it'
'never tell anyone your private business'

whose head was full of paintings
but she gave it all away
for me, for us
as if for a cause

who could burn water
whose pizza was secretly given the dog
and someone caught redhanded

she of Sarah Lee Black Forest reputation
and cigarettes given up
just like that – a power of will

she
of mustn't excite the heart-attack uncle
of the fish fingers, chips
of the steak
and freezer full

she, one of us, once
and the story still telling

she never missed the Scotch
her brothers brought each year for tribute
till one Christmas they asked for a drink

she
whose soul was yours once
hers your unbelief

she
helpless
who forsakes me now

from whom once nothing could ever be hidden
all safe

safe with her
to be home

there isn't the stillness

...is found among neighbours
I mean she is found lurking round the next door flats

won't let them get a word in edgewise

she engages the relatives in mad conversation

she has become a Mohist –
everyone is kin now

she strips off
and slips into their beds
she's surreptitious
if not subtle
don't they get a shock!

she slips out with the visiting party
of course we're, everyone, embarrassed

it's not like she's hard to see

and on the wall
the hour

and in a window
other worlds

and in a word
good night

I introduce her to the flower

where we have been before

valley of some shadow

and go to bed early

in a funk
no one could watch that rubbish

it comes to you and then
not that you can smell it now
but a certain perfume –
a year
and it's gone

flower, mum
mum, flower

I believe that even now she knows
not one of these gifts is from God

the doctor prescribed asthma cigarettes

what do I remember about grandma?

top of the steps
just a shape
mother of mother such

sandstone
pigface
later the cubby leaning
and the under-house

goanna, probably blue tongue

the other one, pink, a little pom-pom like

I only remember just being held

the doctor prescribed asthma cigarettes
that's what she died from

no one'll miss that bastard

never met my grandfather, Billy
died at Wauchope
all be-medalled
below decks most decorated sailor of the war
… that's the story

sad old fuck I suppose
can't know
I never met him

once a year would do the trick
with mum's mum

brought home his syphilitic mate –
                    a last straw

there was a girl in every port

the walk to the pool

and, as I've said (have I?)
    it wouldn't be her swimming
but we were learning

Lady Gowrie's was for convalescence
during the war
and after – was dad there?
Concord Repat

a mile I guess then or a little more
but up hill down dale
decimal, then metric
surely the clocks would be next?

all those dull kangaroos
now some unknown creature shone tiny copper
nickel, metal less than precious

in a heatwave walking, burnt
not even a suburb really then
half bush
sewered blocks carved from the gladioli acre
sandstone blocks
and someone broke an axle on Lynbara
that was the day we moved in

I remember the truck in the mud
and everything coming out
then we were in
it was winter, tucked up
Man from U.N.C.L.E. pyjamas

bright new start
washed all of dad's pipes

you'd think filter cigarettes were some way clean

later threw out my model aeroplane collection
let me not speak of the urine crystals
(Uncle John's idea)

there was the what-to-do-with-the-lottery winnings
but don't forget the disinfectant

that was the closest they came

still birth

something came in
door must have been left
or else no screens

alleged weather
better lock up tight

was he named?
and was this sadness ever said?

miscue
so
left
nothing held

some memories are true

do you remember Elvis?

he pulled you over in the garden
when you broke the first leg

had to be put down

last of the long line

Charming and Cappy 'Captain'
(suppose he was named after Béla)
– the bitey dachshund
died of old age when you were away
but years before
when dad ran over him heading off to work
and you gave him was it port or sherry (?)
by teaspoon
that was a reviver

I buried him, you know
you were in Europe
funny suppose I should talk to you now

the stain on the floor
and the stain on the table

all of my friends were here

the child in the third bedroom

you can't tell ever
how did he get in?

aren't they concerned he's gone?

they say – go with it
always agree
entertain whatever's said

it's the disease that does this
she's not there

it was her wish
not to be like this

is gone the same as where we are?
is lost the same as gone?

High Street

a finger in the harbour
we'd go there to check the paint smell
sun thrown to the frayed floor

scraggle bush
uphill, flower lit
park whichever way

the tall brick past, red then
it was sandstone shade
street ferry ended
hours of the while away

and Aunty Eve's along a bit
where Alice and all those animals
awash but I forgot the tears
that's where they began

had not yet ever come into a book
saw though where they were
left on the page for later
all paws to the moment

were read to, travelled
must have learned forgetting then

up from the carpet
play down to the park
and doggy-do

swing of the picnic
unblaze of blue
the stillnesses of summer so
shining as
little white triangles puff and go
who can you see?
it's a map!

and the bridge glimpse
(various angles)
Greenway building eyesore
and insult to the memory of

kitbag brown and some digits
worn colours ... beginning with the letters NX
like a phone number
from the war before we were

play poker in the smoke
and leave it beery with the march
I must have been essential...
something along the lines of
what it had all been for

High Street was one end of the world
built safe and trudge...
if only you'd bought just after those midget subs

the other way along was weary
because it was *a way*

splash piers of barnacle green
grime harbour

Pinchgut just there for a story
and who was that mad bugger
got between ferry and pier?
every time they had to fish him out

blare azure of up looking
a breeze still
mirror lap nearly
little back forth rocking
shall we call a 'bob'?

paint was always the freshest thing
came over the salt
got a lungful

and back up the hill
of a bit too little
to do the job
but can watch

switching the pictures around
it was a long way up to the ceiling
we were checking up, making sure

wringers in those laundries defunct
from the Depression
(was it really Great?)
they'd have to go
but not today
nor the falling fence

thongs!
and the long grass
cut foot doctor rush
of silly silly mum

like a portrait in the classroom

watching when the teacher is out

I couldn't say hysterectomy then

it was a secret anyway

*

tomorrow is a magpie tells
I'll whisper it to you

that one's mad
shouts
and swoops
it's like being there

something broke on my heart
in this picture
they are when we were
when is he home tonight?

*

I roll away into a ball
roll a ball into
roll into away

*

pearl fishers
will they find?
can you tell?

knit one
and keep the open head
full steam

there's someone can guess the code
but where's that some body now?

let's look into the folds together

and no, again
that's what you say

can't imagine

you're at me now
I know it's you
because you're a *looker*

*

we are outside the study
near where the yellow garden lounge was
though rather over formal for something of such rust
I am saying
yes you have a home
it's not here
but it's the best place for you
you're so much better now
better off

we painted this together
and more than once
in more than one house
I doubt I was much help

I only just remember

*

it was her former wish
never to be in this time beyond

*

those schoolgirls
quite a hoard of them
and princesses Elizabeth

*

a kiss
what's that?
don't touch

*

in a waltz one loses cheek
to river run beside a blue

a kiss is a kind of stealing
a Danube and the violin

*

something is missing
I'll miss you
I'll cry

it's like something's torn out

torn out of you
on good days

you wonder about how much is

*

kind of trance
to think of me
are the Scots all sleeping?
were ancestors too

but it's now right now
10.12
I see it
fancy to meet

dinner comes and goes

*

consider the inevitable
all-tending fate
its brows impression bent will

they were
sisters too suddenly crowned

*

she is no longer messing with my head
I may never recover from this

*

the somebody missing is you

all of the bottles are gone

thinks he's the pope
wowser
took them
wouldn't even have
used to it now
thirsty
I'd just like a drink

I lost my way in the alphabet

among numbers as well

I was skittled
knocked for six

lost my face
your name
way home

it's what you think to look

like putting words
in monkey's truth
at me

I can't say anything of this

but you want to believe that I'm here …
that I'm

I lost the one word left

it was to have been the punchline

the bluetongue

do you remember the day of the bluetongue?
and we thought it was a carving to start
but it was as real as me or you

and chased it into the study
and boxed it under the desk

each of us a little afraid
and the reptile woman came

the carving was still there after
real, like rabbits on the lawn

that look
and who are you?

I know!
you don't say!

gaga

there really isn't an order of things

it wasn't just an hour or two
the whole day vanished
in that room

it's the voices... down the street...

someone was ... and went without saying
        couldn't get a word in

it's disturbing when there's nobody here
no walking out into the snow for this
it's moment to moment
grieve as you go

            found it written all over the house
            on little slips of paper
            the hand a little shaky but as definite as ever

            now it is Thursday
            it's Thursday today

            haven't we been here before?

it's almost as if there were something to mean

        give up on eternal life
        and there's only
        where the clock runs down
        and the mice trip up

eternity's just as far as we are

behold! all things made new

forever's for falling apart

let's spell it out together

these are the mama senryu

what is the thing
I am looking for
where did I leave it last?

hello mum
I have decided to write you
very short poems

you won't need
to remember the last one
or that there will be a next

I can see that
there is no point
to this explanation

I am making
a note
to myself

there's no one in the mirror now

J'ay perdu ma Tourterelle
– Jan Passerat

there's no one in the mirror now
the fear you had forgets its face
there is no sign to show you know

long life's a curse – and will calm come?
blank eyes gaze into blanks of space
there's no one in there now, knock knock!

not this, the pointing lives well past
things missing will forget their name
the fear you had has lost its face

must and must not, vanish truth
and truth is like an hour set stray
there's nothing in the mirror now

the head is emptied out to say
there is no sign could show you know
the growl is all for far away

there's no one in the mirror now
the fear you had forgets its face
there is no sign could show you know
blank eyes in blanks of gazing space

she reaches out for the shining

look into the eyes
of one not there

it's just my forgetting face

I'm putting on the bright
and where did I get that?

there must be one more wonder yet

never a chance of goodbye

vale mum

I put out a general call

clocks set back, winter is coming

we need another tense for this
the still with us in hearts and minds

there is a shift in the fabric

mum was already gone

*

4.30am — you feel in the dark
for the differences

do you know this world? how it will be?
how it can have come about?

it wakes you
like the moment the face presented
something lit, now from the past

everyday objects are else than they are
other shapes to the touch

do you recognize
here is the home still standing
as if not a soul were required?

it comes on
bees loud in the garden of a sun just risen

somewhere a street begins
and it leads everywhere
as if in the story that's telling

familiar words you hear to this day

like lost at the Easter show
and a voice comes over the air
says this is how it is from now
your mother – all mother – is gone

but the callous rest won't even know
get on with the maze to tread

it's as if they were deaf
gone to grey
and nothing will wake them ever again
and nothing will bring them to life

now to be all that she
is was could
fit as a fiddle
a good old stick

because the last is past

character, a card my mum
this Earth must miss

we shine her light on *the subject at hand*
mum that was
will always be

*

now mum is of eternity
whatever, wherever
however that is

we are with her wishes now
soon these ashes, so the sky
over every ocean spread

what if there once were a heaven?
now that heaven's gone

and mum
I celebrate you were
you are with me
and always

www.ingramcontent.com/pod-product-compliance
Lightning Source LLC
Chambersburg PA
CBHW030844090426
42737CB00009B/1098